Tasty Easy Slow Cooker Recipes With Pictures

Shortcut Mouthwatering Meals Cookbook

By Linda Lizzie

Copyright © by Linda Lizzie

Introduction

Welcome to the world of effortless, mouthwatering meals with "Tasty Easy Slow Cooker Recipes With Pictures " by Linda Lizzie. Within the pages of this Kindle book, you will embark on a culinary journey that promises to transform your cooking experience, making it as simple as it is satisfying.

Whether you're a busy professional with little time to spare in the kitchen, a parent looking for nutritious and delicious options for family dinners, or a beginner cook ready to explore the magic of slow cooking, Linda's carefully curated collection of recipes is your perfect companion.

Each recipe in this book has been chosen for its ease, flavor, and comfort it brings to the table. Linda Lizzie's passion for creating approachable, flavorful dishes shines through every page. The best part? Every recipe comes accompanied by a vivid, full-color picture that guides you and inspires you to create the perfect dish.

From savory stews that simmer to perfection while you go about your day to sweet, indulgent desserts that require minimal preparation, "Tasty Easy Slow Cooker Recipes With Pictures" offers diverse dishes to suit every palate and occasion. Linda's tips and tricks will ensure that even the most novice cooks can achieve succulent results every time.

Embrace the joy of stress-free cooking with this recipe collection that promises to keep your slow cooker at the heart of your kitchen. Get ready to set it, forget it, and come home to a warm, welcoming meal that feels like a hug in a bowl.

Prepare to savor each bite and make every meal an occasion to remember with "Tasty Easy Slow Cooker Recipes With Pictures." Let's get cooking!

Table of Contents

Chapter 1: Slow Morning Hearty Breakfasts 6

  01: Oatmeal With Apples.................................6

  02: Broccoli Cheddar Egg Casserole 8

  03: French Cinnamon Toast 10

  04: Banana Walnut Bread Pudding 12

  05: Fried Chicken Breasts Filled 14

  06: Shrimp and Grits....................................16

  07: Pumpkin and Carrot Spice Latte 18

  08: Crispy Tortilla Chips 20

  09: Garlic Creamy Bread 22

  10: Apple Cinnamon Crepes 24

Chapter 2: Midday Savor Slow-Cooked Lunches 26

  11: Grilled Chicken Sandwich 26

  12: Creamy Tuscan Chicken With Pasta.....................28

  13: Minestrone With Sauce...............................30

  14: Thai Red Curry Chicken 32

  15: Chickpea Stew With Spinach 34

  16: Barbecue Beef Brisket 36

  17: Buffalo Chicken Sandwich Wrap 38

  18: Cajun Shrimp Scampi With Rice 40

  19: Chicken Egg Rolls 42

  20: Chicken Zucchini Pasta 44

Chapter 3: Dinner on a Dime Slow Cooker Specialties 46

  21: Pot Roast With Carrots and Potatoes 46

  22: Creamy Garlic Butter Tuscan Salmon...................48

  23: Honey Chicken Thighs Baked 50

  24: Risotto With Mushrooms 52

  25: Maple Glazed Pork Tenderloin 54

  26: Beef Bourguignon Stew 56

27: Thai Green Curry Chicken 58

28: Greek Lemon Chicken With Potatoes 60

29: Duck Breast With Orange Sauce 62

30: Beef Stroganoff 64

Chapter 4: Seafood Siesta Slow Cooker Dishes 66

31: Spicy Lemon Garlic Shrimp 66

32: Scallops With Cauliflower Puree 68

33: Cod Stewed With Vegetables 70

34: Steamed Mussels in Creamy Tomato 72

35: Seafood Gumbo With White Rice 74

36: Spicy Shrimp Tacos With Coleslaw 76

37: Mediterranean Seafood Stew Cioppino 78

38: Southern Crawfish Boil 80

39: Steamed Crabs Fulled 82

40: Parmesan Encrusted Tilapia 84

Chapter 5: Soup's On Slow Cooker Comfort 86

41: Creamy Tomato Basil Soup 86

42: Leeks and Potatoes Soup 88

43: Chicken Noodle Soup 90

44: Butternut Squash Apple Soup 92

45: Creamy Italian Tortellini Wild Rice Soup 94

46: Red Lentils and Tomato Soup 96

47: Beef and Barley Soup 98

48: Corn Chowder Soup With Bacon.........................100

49: Classic French Onion Soup 102

50: Chicken Tortilla Soup 104

Conclusion 106

Chapter 1: Slow Morning Hearty Breakfasts

01: Oatmeal With Apples

Embrace the comforting flavors of fall with this slow cooker oatmeal, combining apples, raisins, and cinnamon for a warm, hearty breakfast.

Servings: 4

Prepping Time: 10 minutes

Cook Time: 6 hours

Difficulty: Easy

Ingredients:

- ➢ 1 cup steel-cut oats
- ➢ 4 cups water
- ➢ 2 apples, peeled, cored and chopped
- ➢ 1/2 cup raisins
- ➢ 1 tsp ground cinnamon
- ➢ 1/4 cup brown sugar
- ➢ 1/2 tsp salt

Step-by-Step Preparation:

1. Add oats and water to the slow cooker.
2. Stir in chopped apples, raisins, cinnamon, brown sugar, and salt.
3. Cover and set the slow cooker to low.
4. Cook for 6 hours, stirring occasionally if possible.
5. Serve warm, and add additional toppings if desired.

Nutritional Facts: (Per serving)

- ❖ Calories: 215
- ❖ Protein: 5g
- ❖ Dietary Fiber: 6g
- ❖ Sugars: 18g
- ❖ Sodium: 300mg

Begin your day with this fuss-free, aromatic oatmeal. Each spoonful is a delightful mix of soft apples, plump raisins, and a hint of cinnamon—a nourishing start worth waking up to.

02: Broccoli Cheddar Egg Casserole

Discover the simplicity and savoriness of a slow cooker breakfast with this Broccoli Cheddar Egg Casserole. Ideal for a stress-free morning, it delivers a comforting and hearty start to your day.

Servings: 4

Prepping Time: 15 minutes

Cook Time: 2-3 hours on high, 4-6 hours on low

Difficulty: Easy

Ingredients:

- ➤ 4 cups of broccoli florets
- ➤ 1 cup shredded cheddar cheese
- ➤ 8 large eggs
- ➤ 1 cup milk
- ➤ 1 teaspoon mustard powder
- ➤ 1/2 teaspoon paprika
- ➤ Salt and pepper to taste
- ➤ Non-stick cooking spray

Step-by-Step Preparation:

1. Spray the slow cooker with non-stick cooking spray.
2. Place the broccoli florets into the slow cooker.
3. In a bowl, whisk together eggs, milk, mustard powder, paprika, salt, and pepper.
4. Pour the egg mixture over the broccoli.
5. Sprinkle shredded cheddar cheese on top.
6. Cover and cook on high for 2-3 hours or on low for 4-6 hours or until eggs are set.
7. Serve warm.

Nutritional Facts: (Per serving)

- ❖ Calories: 320
- ❖ Protein: 22g
- ❖ Carbohydrates: 10g
- ❖ Fat: 22g
- ❖ Fiber: 2g
- ❖ Cholesterol: 390mg
- ❖ Sodium: 420mg

Wrap up your morning prep and let the slow cooker work with this Broccoli Cheddar Egg Casserole. Its cheesy, vegetable-packed goodness makes for a wholesome and fulfilling breakfast that's sure to be a hit with the whole family.

03: French Cinnamon Toast

Indulge in the comforting embrace of French cinnamon toast, layered with the tart sweetness of blueberries and raspberries, drizzled with rich maple syrup, and accompanied by a warm cup of coffee.

Servings: 4

Prepping Time: 15 mins

Cook Time: 2 hours

Difficulty: Easy

Ingredients:

- 8 slices of thick-cut bread
- 4 eggs
- 1 cup of milk
- 1 tsp of cinnamon
- 1 cup of blueberries
- 1 cup of raspberries
- 1/4 cup of maple syrup
- Butter for greasing
- 4 cups of freshly brewed coffee

Step-by-Step Preparation:

1. Grease the slow cooker with butter.
2. In a bowl, whisk together eggs, milk, and cinnamon.
3. Dip each bread slice into the mixture and layer in the slow cooker.
4. Scatter blueberries and raspberries over the bread.
5. Cook on low for 2 hours.
6. Serve with maple syrup drizzled on top and hot coffee.

Nutritional Facts: (Per serving)

- ❖ Calories: 350
- ❖ Protein: 12g
- ❖ Carbohydrates: 52g
- ❖ Fat: 10g
- ❖ Fiber: 4g
- ❖ Sugar: 22g

Ease into your morning with a leisurely breakfast slowly simmering to perfection. French cinnamon toast with berries and syrup becomes a symphony of flavors that makes your first meal of the day feel like a weekend treat, any day of the week.

04: Banana Walnut Bread Pudding

Indulge in the warm, comforting embrace of banana walnut bread pudding, a delightful twist on a classic that transforms your breakfast into a gourmet experience straight from your slow cooker.

Servings: 4

Prepping Time: 15 minutes

Cook Time: 4 hours

Difficulty: Easy

Ingredients:

- 4 cups of day-old bread, cubed
- 2 ripe bananas, mashed
- 1/3 cup walnuts, chopped
- 2 cups whole milk
- 2 large eggs
- 1/4 cup brown sugar
- 1 teaspoon vanilla extract
- 1/2 teaspoon cinnamon
- 1/4 teaspoon nutmeg

➢ A pinch of salt

Step-by-Step Preparation:

1. Lightly grease the inside of your slow cooker.
2. Place the bread cubes at the bottom.
3. In a bowl, mix mashed bananas and walnuts, then spread over the bread.
4. Whisk together milk, eggs, brown sugar, vanilla, cinnamon, nutmeg, and salt.
5. Pour the mixture over the bread, ensuring all pieces are coated.
6. Cook on low for 4 hours until the pudding is set and the top is golden brown.

Nutritional Facts: (Per serving)

❖ Calories: 350
❖ Protein: 9g
❖ Carbohydrates: 45g
❖ Fat: 15g
❖ Fiber: 3g
❖ Cholesterol: 96mg
❖ Sodium: 260mg

As the aroma of vanilla and cinnamon fills your kitchen, a slice of this banana walnut bread pudding becomes the perfect start to your day. Linger over each spoonful, and let the slow cooker do the magic while you savor your morning moments.

05: Fried Chicken Breasts Filled

Indulge in the comforting flavors of fried chicken breasts stuffed with a creamy cheese blend and spinach; all simmered to perfection in a savory sauce. This slow cooker recipe promises a delightful breakfast treat for the senses.

Servings: 4

Prepping Time: 20 minutes

Cook Time: 3 hours

Difficulty: Medium

Ingredients:

> 4 boneless, skinless chicken breasts
> 1 cup of fresh spinach, chopped
> 1 cup of shredded cheese (cheddar or mozzarella)
> 1 teaspoon of garlic powder
> 1 teaspoon of paprika
> Salt and pepper to taste
> 1 tablespoon of olive oil
> 2 cups of your favorite creamy sauce (alfredo, garlic cream, etc.)

Step-by-Step Preparation:

1. Flatten chicken breasts to about 1/4 inch thickness.
2. Season both sides with garlic powder, paprika, salt, and pepper.
3. Lay the spinach and cheese on one side of each breast and roll tightly.
4. Secure with toothpicks and lightly brown in olive oil in a skillet.
5. Place the rolls in the slow cooker and cover with sauce.
6. Cook on low for about 3 hours or until chicken is cooked through.

Nutritional Facts: (Per serving)

- ❖ Calories: 350
- ❖ Protein: 31g
- ❖ Carbohydrates: 8g
- ❖ Fat: 21g
- ❖ Cholesterol: 90mg
- ❖ Sodium: 690mg

Savor the tender chicken encasing a gooey center of cheese and spinach, all infused with a rich sauce that turns a simple meal into a memorable feast. This slow cooker dish brings gourmet breakfast to your table with minimal fuss and maximum flavor.

06: Shrimp and Grits

Savor the Southern comfort of shrimp and grits, effortlessly prepared in your slow cooker. This hearty breakfast will awaken your taste buds and warm your soul.

Servings: 4

Prepping Time: 15 minutes

Cook Time: 6 hours

Difficulty: Easy

Ingredients:

- 1 cup stone-ground grits
- 4 cups water
- 1 teaspoon salt
- 1/2 teaspoon black pepper
- 1 pound raw shrimp, peeled and deveined
- 1 cup cheddar cheese, shredded
- 1/4 cup butter
- 1/2 cup heavy cream
- 1 teaspoon paprika

> ➤ 4 slices of bacon, cooked and crumbled
> ➤ 2 green onions, thinly sliced

Step-by-Step Preparation:

1. Rinse grits under cold water and drain.
2. Combine grits, water, and salt in the slow cooker.
3. Cook on low for 5 to 6 hours until grits are soft.
4. Stir in black pepper, cheese, butter, and heavy cream until well combined.
5. Add the raw shrimp and paprika in the last 30 minutes of cooking.
6. Top with bacon and green onions before serving.

Nutritional Facts: (Per serving)

- ❖ Calories: 540
- ❖ Protein: 35g
- ❖ Carbohydrates: 48g
- ❖ Fat: 24g
- ❖ Cholesterol: 220mg
- ❖ Sodium: 970mg
- ❖ Fiber: 2g

Experience a delightful start to your day with this creamy, comforting bowl of shrimp and grits. It's the perfect slow cooker dish to bring a touch of Southern charm to your breakfast table.

07: Pumpkin and Carrot Spice Latte

Embrace the cozy essence of fall with this heartwarming pumpkin and carrot spice latte. It's a perfect slow cooker breakfast that fills your home with inviting aromas and warms you from the inside out.

Servings: 4

Prepping Time: 15 minutes

Cook Time: 2 hours

Difficulty: Easy

Ingredients:

- ➢ 2 cups milk
- ➢ 1/2 cup pumpkin puree
- ➢ 1/4 cup finely grated carrots
- ➢ 1/4 cup strong coffee or espresso
- ➢ 1/2 teaspoon vanilla extract
- ➢ 1/4 teaspoon ground cinnamon, plus extra for garnish
- ➢ 1/8 teaspoon ground nutmeg
- ➢ 1/8 teaspoon ground ginger
- ➢ 2 tablespoons maple syrup

> ➤ Whipped cream for serving

Step-by-Step Preparation:

1. Combine milk, pumpkin puree, grated carrots, coffee, vanilla extract, cinnamon, nutmeg, ginger, and maple syrup in the slow cooker.
2. Stir well to ensure the mixture is thoroughly combined.
3. Cover and cook on low for 2 hours, stirring occasionally.
4. After 2 hours, whisk the latte to create a frothy texture.
5. Serve hot with a dollop of whipped cream and a sprinkle of cinnamon on top.

Nutritional Facts: (Per serving)

- ❖ Calories: 150
- ❖ Protein: 5g
- ❖ Carbohydrates: 24g
- ❖ Fat: 3.5g
- ❖ Sugar: 20g
- ❖ Sodium: 105mg

Sip, savor, and indulge in the seasonal delight of this pumpkin and carrot spice latte. A creamy, frothy beverage that not only satisfies your taste buds but also offers a nourishing start to your day. Let this slow cooker specialty become a cherished part of your autumn mornings.

08: Crispy Tortilla Chips

Wake up to the comforting aroma of crispy tortilla chips layered with melted cheddar, zesty salsa, and all your favorite toppings, all conveniently prepared in your slow cooker.

Servings: 4

Prepping Time: 15 minutes

Cook Time: 2 hours

Difficulty: Easy

Ingredients:

- ➢ 4 large flour tortillas
- ➢ 1 cup cheddar cheese, shredded
- ➢ 1 cup salsa
- ➢ 1/2 cup black beans, rinsed and drained
- ➢ 1/4 cup jalapenos, sliced
- ➢ 1/2 cup guacamole
- ➢ 1/2 cup sour cream
- ➢ 1/2 cup lettuce, shredded

Step-by-Step Preparation:

1. Cut tortillas into chip-sized pieces and layer at the bottom of the slow cooker.
2. Sprinkle half of the shredded cheddar over the tortillas.
3. Spread the salsa and black beans evenly over the cheese.
4. Add another layer of tortilla chips and the remaining cheddar.
5. Cook on low for 2 hours.
6. Once cooked, top with jalapenos, dollops of guacamole, sour cream, and shredded lettuce.

Nutritional Facts: (Per serving)

- ❖ Calories: 350
- ❖ Protein: 12g
- ❖ Carbohydrates: 34g
- ❖ Fat: 20g
- ❖ Fiber: 5g
- ❖ Sodium: 680mg

Enjoy this symphony of flavors as your new morning tradition, a slow-cooked delight that infuses your breakfast with a festive spirit. It's like a morning fiesta on a plate, just waiting to energize your day.

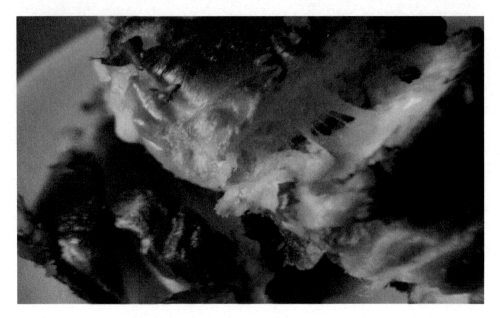

09: Garlic Creamy Bread

Embark on a culinary journey with this Garlic Creamy Bread, a sumptuous slow cooker breakfast that effortlessly melds the rich flavors of garlic and cream.

Servings: 4

Prepping Time: 15 mins

Cook Time: 2 Hours on low

Difficulty: Easy

Ingredients:

- 1 French baguette, sliced into 1-inch pieces
- 4 cloves of garlic, minced
- 1 cup heavy cream
- 1 cup whole milk
- 1/2 cup grated Parmesan cheese
- 1/2 tsp salt
- 1/4 tsp black pepper
- 2 tbsp fresh parsley, chopped
- 1/2 cup shredded mozzarella cheese

Step-by-Step Preparation:

1. Combine garlic, cream, milk, Parmesan, salt, and pepper in a bowl.
2. Arrange bread slices in the slow cooker.
3. Pour the cream mixture over the bread, ensuring all pieces are coated.
4. Cover and cook on low for 2 hours.
5. Sprinkle with mozzarella and parsley in the last 10 minutes.
6. Serve once the cheese is melted and bubbly.

Nutritional Facts: (Per serving)

- ❖ Calories: 410
- ❖ Total Fat: 27g
- ❖ Saturated Fat: 16g
- ❖ Cholesterol: 89mg
- ❖ Sodium: 780mg
- ❖ Total Carbohydrates: 31g
- ❖ Dietary Fiber: 1g
- ❖ Sugars: 5g
- ❖ Protein: 14g

Experience the delightful blend of aromatic garlic and luscious cream with every bite of this simple yet sophisticated Garlic Creamy Bread, crafted to warm your mornings and bring gourmet to your breakfast table.

10: Apple Cinnamon Crepes

Savor the warmth of apple cinnamon crepes, a slow cooker delight that marries the coziness of cinnamon with the sweetness of apples in a delicate crepe.

Servings: 4

Prepping Time: 20 minutes

Cook Time: 2 hours 30 minutes

Difficulty: Medium

Ingredients:

- ➢ 1 cup all-purpose flour
- ➢ 2 eggs
- ➢ 1/2 cup milk
- ➢ 1/2 cup water
- ➢ 2 tbsp melted butter
- ➢ 1/4 tsp salt
- ➢ 2 apples, thinly sliced
- ➢ 1 tsp ground cinnamon
- ➢ 2 tbsp brown sugar

➤ 1 tbsp lemon juice
➤ Powdered sugar for garnish

Step-by-Step Preparation:

1. In a large bowl, whisk together flour, eggs, milk, water, melted butter, and salt until smooth.
2. In the slow cooker, combine sliced apples, cinnamon, brown sugar, and lemon juice.
3. Pour the crepe batter over the apple mixture in the slow cooker.
4. Cook on low for 2 to 2.5 hours until edges are lightly browned.
5. Carefully remove crepes and serve with a dusting of powdered sugar.

Nutritional Facts: (Per serving)

❖ Calories: 235
❖ Protein: 6g
❖ Carbohydrates: 40g
❖ Fat: 6g
❖ Fiber: 2g
❖ Sugar: 15g

Wrap up your morning with the lingering sweetness and spice of apple cinnamon crepes. This easy yet impressive slow cooker recipe provides a delicious twist to your breakfast, leaving you satisfied and ready to start the day.

Chapter 2: Midday Savor Slow-Cooked Lunches

11: Grilled Chicken Sandwich

Discover the perfect harmony of flavors in this slow cooker grilled chicken sandwich topped with melted mozzarella and a tangy balsamic vinaigrette dressing. Ideal for a leisurely lunch, this recipe offers a gourmet twist on a classic.

Servings: 4

Prepping Time: 15 minutes

Cook Time: 4 hours

Difficulty: Easy

Ingredients:

- ➢ 4 boneless, skinless chicken breasts
- ➢ 1 teaspoon garlic powder
- ➢ Salt and pepper to taste
- ➢ 4 slices of mozzarella cheese

- ➢ 4 whole-grain sandwich buns
- ➢ 1 cup balsamic vinaigrette dressing
- ➢ 1 tablespoon olive oil
- ➢ 2 tomatoes, sliced
- ➢ 1 small red onion, thinly sliced
- ➢ 1 cup fresh arugula

Step-by-Step Preparation:

1. Season chicken with garlic powder, salt, and pepper.
2. Place chicken in slow cooker and drizzle with olive oil.
3. Pour balsamic vinaigrette over the chicken.
4. Cover and cook on high for 4 hours.
5. In the last 10 minutes, place a slice of mozzarella on each chicken breast.
6. Toast buns lightly, if desired.
7. Assemble sandwiches with chicken, mozzarella, tomato, onion, and arugula.
8. Drizzle with additional balsamic vinaigrette to taste.

Nutritional Facts: (Per serving)

- ❖ Calories: 580
- ❖ Protein: 35g
- ❖ Carbohydrates: 46g
- ❖ Fat: 26g
- ❖ Cholesterol: 95mg
- ❖ Sodium: 870mg
- ❖ Fiber: 3g

Savor each bite of this slow-cooked, succulent chicken sandwich, enhanced by the melting mozzarella and the zesty balsamic dressing.

12: Creamy Tuscan Chicken With Pasta

Indulge in the rich flavors of Italy with this creamy Tuscan chicken paired with perfectly cooked pasta. The meal that promises to transport your taste buds. The heart of Tuscany, all with the convenience of your slow cooker.

Servings: 4

Prepping Time: 15 minutes

Cook Time: 4 hours on low

Difficulty: Easy

Ingredients:

- ➤ 4 boneless, skinless chicken breasts
- ➤ 1 teaspoon garlic powder
- ➤ 1 tablespoon Italian seasoning
- ➤ Salt and pepper to taste
- ➤ 1 cup heavy cream
- ➤ ½ cup chicken broth
- ➤ ⅓ cup sun-dried tomatoes, chopped
- ➤ 2 cups spinach, roughly chopped
- ➤ 1 cup grated Parmesan cheese

➢ 8 ounces pasta, cooked al dente

Step-by-Step Preparation:

1. Season chicken breasts with garlic powder, Italian seasoning, salt, and pepper; place in the slow cooker.
2. Pour in chicken broth and heavy cream; stir to combine.
3. Add sun-dried tomatoes on top of the chicken.
4. Cover and cook on low for 4 hours.
5. In the last 30 minutes of cooking, add spinach and Parmesan cheese; stir into the sauce.
6. Prepare pasta according to package instructions; drain.
7. Shred the chicken in the slow cooker and mix with the creamy sauce.
8. Serve the creamy chicken over cooked pasta, and enjoy.

Nutritional Facts: (Per serving)

❖ Calories: 650
❖ Protein: 35g
❖ Carbohydrates: 54g
❖ Fat: 32g
❖ Saturated Fat: 18g
❖ Cholesterol: 165mg
❖ Sodium: 710mg
❖ Fiber: 3g
❖ Sugar: 4g

After savoring each forkful of this decadent Creamy Tuscan Chicken with Pasta, you'll appreciate the effortless elegance it adds to your lunch repertoire. This slow cooker recipe not only simplifies cooking but also brings a piece of the Tuscan sun to your table.

13: Minestrone With Sauce

Immerse yourself in the robust flavors of a classic Italian soup with this slow cooker minestrone with sauce. Perfect for a comforting lunch, it blends hearty vegetables, beans, and pasta in a savory tomato base.

Servings: 4

Prepping Time: 15 minutes

Cook Time: 6 hours on low

Difficulty: Easy

Ingredients:

- ➤ 1 can diced tomatoes
- ➤ 1 can white beans, drained and rinsed
- ➤ 2 carrots, chopped
- ➤ 2 stalks celery, chopped
- ➤ 1 medium onion, diced
- ➤ 2 cloves garlic, minced
- ➤ 4 cups vegetable broth
- ➤ 1 tsp dried oregano
- ➤ 1 tsp dried basil

- ➢ 1 bay leaf
- ➢ 1 cup ditalini pasta
- ➢ Salt and pepper to taste
- ➢ 2 cups spinach leaves
- ➢ Parmesan cheese, for garnish

Step-by-Step Preparation:

1. Place the tomatoes, beans, carrots, celery, onion, and garlic into the slow cooker.
2. Pour the vegetable broth and stir in the oregano, basil, and bay leaf.
3. Cover and cook on low for 5 to 6 hours until vegetables are tender.
4. In the last 30 minutes of cooking, add the ditalini pasta and spinach.
5. Season with salt and pepper, then remove the bay leaf before serving.
6. Serve hot, garnished with grated Parmesan cheese.

Nutritional Facts: (Per serving)

- ❖ Calories: 250
- ❖ Protein: 12g
- ❖ Carbohydrates: 45g
- ❖ Dietary Fiber: 10g
- ❖ Sugars: 6g
- ❖ Fat: 2g
- ❖ Saturated Fat: 0.5g
- ❖ Sodium: 700mg

As the minestrone warms you from the inside, the ease of this slow cooker recipe frees up your time. Relish in the simplicity of a meal that offers a symphony of veggies, beans, and pasta, culminating in a nourishing experience for both body and soul.

14: Thai Red Curry Chicken

Immerse yourself in the flavors of Thailand with this sumptuous slow cooker Thai red curry chicken featuring the unique taste of pea eggplants. A perfect meld of spices and juiciness, this dish promises a culinary escape right in your kitchen.

Servings: 4

Prepping Time: 15 Minutes

Cook Time: 4 Hours

Difficulty: Medium

Ingredients:

- ➢ 1 lb chicken thighs, cut into pieces
- ➢ 2 tablespoons Thai red curry paste
- ➢ 1 can of coconut milk
- ➢ 1 cup pea eggplants
- ➢ 1 tablespoon fish sauce
- ➢ 1 teaspoon brown sugar
- ➢ 1 red bell pepper, sliced
- ➢ 1 tablespoon vegetable oil

- ➢ 1/2 cup chicken broth
- ➢ Fresh basil leaves for garnish
- ➢ Salt to taste

Step-by-Step Preparation:

1. Heat oil in a skillet over medium heat and brown the chicken pieces.
2. Transfer the chicken to the slow cooker.
3. In the same skillet, sauté the red curry paste until fragrant.
4. Stir in coconut milk, fish sauce, brown sugar, and chicken broth, bringing it to a simmer.
5. Pour the sauce over the chicken in the slow cooker.
6. Add pea eggplants and red bell pepper to the mixture.
7. Cook on low for 4 hours until the chicken is tender.
8. Season with salt to taste and garnish with fresh basil before serving.

Nutritional Facts: (Per serving)

- ❖ Calories: 350
- ❖ Protein: 28g
- ❖ Carbohydrates: 15g
- ❖ Fat: 20g
- ❖ Saturated Fat: 12g
- ❖ Cholesterol: 80mg
- ❖ Sodium: 750mg
- ❖ Fiber: 3g
- ❖ Sugar: 5g

Wrap up your culinary adventure with this heartwarming Thai red curry chicken. As the slow cooker works its magic, the chicken and pea eggplants soak up the coconut-infused sauce, delivering tender bites full of exotic flavor – a satisfying lunch that will transport you to the heart of Thailand.

15: Chickpea Stew With Spinach

Discover the heartwarming comfort of a slow-cooked Chickpea stew with spinach and cod, a traditional Spanish potaje de vigilia. This dish marries the richness of chickpeas with tender cod and fresh spinach for a hearty lunchtime feast.

Servings: 4

Prepping Time: 20 minutes

Cook Time: 6 hours

Difficulty: Medium

Ingredients:

- 1 cup dried chickpeas, soaked overnight
- 4 cod fillets
- 2 cups fresh spinach
- 1 large onion, chopped
- 2 garlic cloves, minced
- 1 teaspoon smoked paprika
- 1 bay leaf
- 4 cups vegetable broth

➢ 2 tablespoons olive oil
➢ Salt and pepper to taste

Step-by-Step Preparation:

1. Rinse and drain the soaked chickpeas.
2. In the slow cooker, layer the chickpeas, onion, garlic, smoked paprika, and bay leaf.
3. Pour in the vegetable broth, ensuring the chickpeas are fully submerged.
4. Cook on low for 5 hours.
5. Season the cod fillets with salt and pepper and place on top of the chickpeas.
6. Add the fresh spinach and drizzle with olive oil.
7. Cook for an additional hour or until the cod is flaky and the chickpeas are tender.
8. Adjust seasoning and serve warm.

Nutritional Facts: (Per serving)

❖ Calories: 380
❖ Protein: 35g
❖ Carbohydrates: 45g
❖ Fiber: 10g
❖ Fat: 9g
❖ Sodium: 300mg

As the slow cooker gently melds the flavors of chickpeas, cod, and spinach, each spoonful of this potage de vigilia becomes a testament to the simple yet profound pleasure of traditional Spanish cuisine. Perfect for a nourishing lunch, this stew promises to satisfy with every bite.

16: Barbecue Beef Brisket

Savor the rich flavors of Texas with this succulent slow cooker barbecue beef brisket. Perfect for a hearty lunch, this tender, smoky dish will transport your taste buds straight to the heart of the Lone Star State.

Servings: 4

Prepping Time: 15 minutes

Cook Time: 8 hours

Difficulty: Medium

Ingredients:

> ➢ 2 lbs beef brisket
> ➢ 2 tbsp brown sugar
> ➢ 1 tbsp smoked paprika
> ➢ 2 tsp garlic powder
> ➢ 2 tsp onion powder
> ➢ 1 tsp cayenne pepper
> ➢ Salt and black pepper to taste
> ➢ 1 cup barbecue sauce
> ➢ 1/2 cup beef broth

- ➢ 2 tbsp Worcestershire sauce
- ➢ 1 tbsp olive oil

Step-by-Step Preparation:

1. Mix brown sugar, smoked paprika, garlic powder, onion powder, cayenne pepper, salt, and black pepper in a bowl.
2. Rub the spice mixture all over the brisket.
3. Heat olive oil in a skillet and sear brisket on both sides until browned.
4. Place the brisket in the slow cooker.
5. Combine barbecue sauce, beef broth, and Worcestershire sauce; pour over the brisket.
6. Set the slow cooker to low and cook for 8 hours until tender.
7. Remove brisket, rest for 10 minutes, then slice or shred.
8. Serve with the sauce from the slow cooker drizzled on top.

Nutritional Facts: (Per serving)

- ❖ Calories: 480
- ❖ Protein: 35g
- ❖ Carbohydrates: 18g
- ❖ Fat: 29g
- ❖ Saturated Fat: 10g
- ❖ Cholesterol: 105mg
- ❖ Sodium: 850mg
- ❖ Fiber: 1g
- ❖ Sugar: 12g

After eight hours of slow cooking, your Texas-style barbecue beef brisket is ready to be the star of your lunch table. With a balance of sweet and spicy, every tender slice is a nod to traditional Southern barbecues. Gather around, share, and enjoy this comforting meal with friends or family.

17: Buffalo Chicken Sandwich Wrap

Spice up your lunch with this mouthwatering slow-cooker buffalo chicken sandwich wrap. Filled with juicy chicken, tangy bleu cheese, and crisp romaine lettuce, it's a flavorful meal that's sure to please.

Servings: 4

Prepping Time: 20 minutes

Cook Time: 4 hours

Difficulty: Easy

Ingredients:

- ➢ 4 boneless, skinless chicken breasts
- ➢ 1 cup buffalo wing sauce
- ➢ 4 large flour tortillas
- ➢ 1 head romaine lettuce, shredded
- ➢ 1/2 cup bleu cheese crumbles
- ➢ 1 cup ranch dressing
- ➢ 1 tablespoon olive oil
- ➢ Salt and pepper to taste
- ➢ 1 bag of frozen fries for serving

Step-by-Step Preparation:

1. Place the chicken breasts in the slow cooker and pour buffalo wing sauce over them. Cook on low for 4 hours.
2. Once cooked, shred the chicken in the sauce.
3. Preheat oven and bake fries according to package instructions.
4. Lay out the tortillas and evenly distribute the lettuce and bleu cheese on each.
5. Top with the shredded buffalo chicken and drizzle with ranch dressing.
6. Roll up the tortillas tightly into wraps, securing them with toothpicks if needed.
7. Cut each wrap in half and serve with a side of crispy fries.

Nutritional Facts: (Per serving)

- ❖ Calories: 650
- ❖ Protein: 38g
- ❖ Carbohydrates: 58g
- ❖ Fat: 29g
- ❖ Cholesterol: 95mg
- ❖ Sodium: 2150mg

After savoring the tangy and spicy flavors of this buffalo chicken wrap, you'll find it hard to believe it was so simple to make. This slow cooker lunch dish, paired with crispy fries, is not only satisfying but also a surefire hit for any day of the week.

18: Cajun Shrimp Scampi With Rice

Dive into the bold flavors of the South with this Cajun Shrimp Scampi. This slow cooker dish marries Creole spices with classic scampi sauce, served over fluffy rice for a comforting lunchtime feast.

Servings: 4

Prepping Time: 15 minutes

Cook Time: 2 hours

Difficulty: Easy

Ingredients:

- ➤ 1 lb large shrimp, peeled and deveined
- ➤ 1 cup white rice
- ➤ 2 tablespoons Cajun seasoning
- ➤ 3 cloves garlic, minced
- ➤ 1/4 cup chicken broth
- ➤ 1/4 cup white wine
- ➤ 2 tablespoons lemon juice
- ➤ 4 tablespoons unsalted butter
- ➤ 1/4 cup chopped parsley

➢ Salt and pepper to taste

Step-by-Step Preparation:

1. Season shrimp with Cajun spices and set aside.
2. Rinse rice and place in the slow cooker with chicken broth and a pinch of salt.
3. In a pan, sauté garlic in butter, then add white wine and lemon juice to make the scampi sauce.
4. Pour the sauce over the shrimp and add to the slow cooker.
5. Cook on low for 2 hours.
6. Stir in parsley before serving over rice.

Nutritional Facts: (Per serving)

❖ Calories: 350
❖ Protein: 24g
❖ Carbohydrates: 45g
❖ Fat: 8g
❖ Sodium: 870mg
❖ Cholesterol: 180mg

Savor each bite of this slow-cooked Cajun Shrimp Scampi, a dish that brings the spirit of Creole cuisine right to your table. Perfect for those who love a kick of spice and the heartiness of a home-cooked meal, this recipe promises to delight your palate and warm your soul.

19: Chicken Egg Rolls

Immerse yourself in the savory world of slow-cooked chicken egg rolls, a perfect fusion of tender chicken and crisp vegetables wrapped in a golden-brown shell.

Servings: 4

Prepping Time: 20 mins

Cook Time: 4 hours

Difficulty: Medium

Ingredients:

- ➤ 2 cups shredded cooked chicken
- ➤ 1 cup shredded cabbage
- ➤ 1/2 cup grated carrots
- ➤ 1/4 cup finely chopped green onions
- ➤ 2 garlic cloves, minced
- ➤ 1 tbsp soy sauce
- ➤ 1 tsp sesame oil
- ➤ 1/4 tsp ground ginger
- ➤ 8 egg roll wrappers

➤ 1 tbsp cornstarch mixed with 2 tbsp water
➤ Cooking spray

Step-by-Step Preparation:

1. Combine chicken, cabbage, carrots, green onions, garlic, soy sauce, sesame oil, and ginger in a bowl.
2. Place an egg roll wrapper on a clean surface, point facing you. Spoon 1/4 of the mixture onto the wrapper.
3. Fold in the sides and roll tightly, sealing the end with cornstarch.
4. Repeat with remaining wrappers and filling.
5. Spray the inside of the slow cooker with cooking spray and place the egg rolls inside.
6. Cook on low for 4 hours until the rolls are heated through and slightly crispy.

Nutritional Facts: (Per serving)

❖ Calories: 350
❖ Protein: 25g
❖ Carbohydrates: 35g
❖ Fat: 10g
❖ Sodium: 620mg
❖ Fiber: 2g

Delight your palate with these delectably slow-cooked chicken egg rolls that blend the convenience of a crockpot with the classic crunch and flavor of this beloved dish.

20: Chicken Zucchini Pasta

Embark on a flavorful journey with this Chicken Zucchini Pasta enveloped in a homemade tomato sauce. Let your slow cooker do the magic, blending herbs and spices to perfection for a heartwarming lunch.

Servings: 4

Prepping Time: 15 minutes

Cook Time: 4 hours

Difficulty: Easy

Ingredients:

- ➢ 2 large chicken breasts, cut into chunks
- ➢ 4 medium zucchini, spiralized
- ➢ 1 (24-ounce) jar tomato sauce
- ➢ 1 onion, finely chopped
- ➢ 2 cloves garlic, minced
- ➢ 1 teaspoon dried oregano
- ➢ 1 teaspoon dried basil
- ➢ Salt and pepper to taste
- ➢ 2 tablespoons olive oil

> ➢ 1/4 cup grated Parmesan cheese (optional for garnish)

Step-by-Step Preparation:

1. Heat the olive oil over medium heat and brown the chicken chunks until golden.
2. Place the browned chicken in the slow cooker.
3. Sauté the chopped onion and minced garlic in the same pan until translucent and fragrant. Add to the slow cooker.
4. Pour the tomato sauce over the chicken. Stir in oregano, basil, salt, and pepper.
5. Cover and cook on low for 4 hours.
6. In the last 30 minutes of cooking, add the spiralized zucchini to the slow cooker.
7. Stir gently to combine, cover, and cook until the zucchini is tender.
8. Serve hot, garnished with Parmesan cheese if desired.

Nutritional Facts: (Per serving)

- ❖ Calories: 320
- ❖ Protein: 27g
- ❖ Carbohydrates: 18g
- ❖ Fat: 14g
- ❖ Fiber: 4g
- ❖ Sodium: 470mg

As the last spoonful of this delectable Chicken Zucchini Pasta with Tomato Sauce lingers on your palate, you'll revel in the knowledge that this slow-cooked wonder has not only satisfied your cravings but has nourished your body with wholesome goodness.

Chapter 3: Dinner on a Dime Slow Cooker Specialties

21: Pot Roast With Carrots and Potatoes

Indulge in the heartwarming flavors of a classic slow cooker pot roast, tenderly cooked with carrots and potatoes. This effortless meal melds savory herbs and veggies for a comforting dinner.

Servings: 4

Prepping Time: 15 minutes

Cook Time: 8 hours

Difficulty: Easy

Ingredients:

- ➢ 2 lbs beef chuck roast
- ➢ 4 large carrots, cut into chunks
- ➢ 3 large potatoes, quartered
- ➢ 1 onion, sliced
- ➢ 4 cloves garlic, minced

- ➢ 2 cups beef broth
- ➢ 1 tbsp Worcestershire sauce
- ➢ 2 tsp salt
- ➢ 1 tsp black pepper
- ➢ 1 tsp dried thyme
- ➢ 2 tbsp olive oil

Step-by-Step Preparation:

1. Season the beef with salt and pepper and brown it in olive oil over high heat.
2. Place the browned beef in the slow cooker.
3. Add the carrots, potatoes, onion, and garlic around the meat.
4. Pour the beef broth and Worcestershire sauce over the ingredients.
5. Sprinkle with dried thyme.
6. Cover and cook on low for 8 hours until the meat is tender.

Nutritional Facts: (Per serving)

- ❖ Calories: 600
- ❖ Protein: 48g
- ❖ Carbohydrates: 38g
- ❖ Fat: 28g
- ❖ Sodium: 950mg
- ❖ Fiber: 5g

Savor the simplicity and richness of this pot roast, a dish that promises to satisfy your cravings with minimal preparation. Perfect for busy days, it offers a nutritious, hearty meal that the whole family can enjoy.

22: Creamy Garlic Butter Tuscan Salmon

Dive into the heart of Italy with this slow cooker Creamy Garlic Butter Tuscan Salmon. A symphony of flavors featuring salmon, sun-drenched tomatoes, and tender broccoli, all wrapped in a luxurious cream sauce.

Servings: 4

Prepping Time: 15 minutes

Cook Time: 4 hours

Difficulty: Medium

Ingredients:

- ➢ 4 salmon fillets
- ➢ 1 cup heavy cream
- ➢ 2 tbsp garlic, minced
- ➢ 1/2 cup Parmesan cheese, grated
- ➢ 1 cup cherry tomatoes, halved
- ➢ 2 cups broccoli florets
- ➢ 1 tbsp Italian seasoning
- ➢ Salt and pepper to taste
- ➢ 1 tbsp olive oil

Step-by-Step Preparation:

1. Place the salmon fillets at the bottom of the slow cooker.
2. In a bowl, mix heavy cream, garlic, Parmesan, Italian seasoning, salt, and pepper.
3. Pour the mixture over the salmon.
4. Scatter the cherry tomatoes and broccoli around the salmon.
5. Drizzle with olive oil.
6. Cook on low for 4 hours or until salmon flakes easily with a fork.

Nutritional Facts: (Per serving)

❖ Calories: 490
❖ Protein: 34g
❖ Carbohydrates: 8g
❖ Fat: 36g
❖ Saturated Fat: 18g
❖ Cholesterol: 145mg
❖ Sodium: 390mg

Unveil a dish that whispers the secrets of Tuscan kitchens with each savory bite. This Creamy Garlic Butter Tuscan Salmon turns your dinner table into a celebration of comfort and flavor, effortlessly created in your slow cooker.

23: Honey Chicken Thighs Baked

Savor the sweet and savory blend of honey chicken thighs, complemented by the lushness of ripe figs, the tang of mustard, and a medley of herbs in this slow cooker creation designed to tantalize your taste buds with minimal fuss.

Servings: 4

Prepping Time: 15 minutes

Cook Time: 4 hours

Difficulty: Easy

Ingredients:

- ➤ 4 chicken thighs, bone-in, skin-on
- ➤ 8 ripe figs, quartered
- ➤ 1/4 cup honey
- ➤ 2 tablespoons Dijon mustard
- ➤ 3 garlic cloves, minced
- ➤ 1 teaspoon dried thyme
- ➤ 1 teaspoon dried rosemary
- ➤ Salt and pepper to taste
- ➤ 1 tablespoon olive oil

Step-by-Step Preparation:

1. Season chicken thighs with salt, pepper, thyme, and rosemary.
2. Place chicken in the slow cooker.
3. In a bowl, combine honey, mustard, and garlic.
4. Pour the mixture over the chicken.
5. Tuck fig quarters around the chicken.
6. Drizzle olive oil over the top.
7. Cook on low for 4 hours until chicken is tender.

Nutritional Facts: (Per serving)

- ❖ Calories: 350
- ❖ Protein: 25g
- ❖ Carbohydrates: 27g
- ❖ Fat: 16g
- ❖ Fiber: 3g
- ❖ Sugar: 24g

Delight in the ease and comfort of this honey chicken and figs dish. Whether it's a weeknight dinner or a special occasion, the harmony of flavors will make this slow cooker meal a memorable feast for the senses.

24: Risotto With Mushrooms

Discover the creamy goodness of slow cooker risotto, enriched with earthy mushrooms, aromatic fresh herbs, and a generous sprinkle of parmesan cheese. This dish promises to deliver the comfort of Italian cuisine right to your table with minimal effort.

Servings: 4

Prepping Time: 15 minutes

Cook Time: 2 hours

Difficulty: Medium

Ingredients:

- ➤ 1 cup Arborio rice
- ➤ 3 cups chicken or vegetable broth
- ➤ 1 cup fresh mushrooms, sliced
- ➤ 1 small onion, finely chopped
- ➤ 2 cloves garlic, minced
- ➤ 1/4 cup fresh parsley, chopped
- ➤ 1/4 cup fresh basil, chopped
- ➤ 1/2 cup grated parmesan cheese

- ➤ 2 tablespoons olive oil
- ➤ Salt and pepper to taste

Step-by-Step Preparation:

1. In the slow cooker, combine olive oil, onion, and garlic. Set on high and cook until softened.
2. Stir in Arborio rice, ensuring it's well-coated with the oil.
3. Add the mushrooms, broth, salt, and pepper.
4. Cover and cook on low for 2 hours until the rice is tender and creamy.
5. In the last 10 minutes of cooking, stir in the fresh herbs.
6. Once done, sprinkle with grated parmesan cheese and serve.

Nutritional Facts: (Per serving)

- ❖ Calories: 320
- ❖ Protein: 9g
- ❖ Carbohydrates: 48g
- ❖ Fat: 9g
- ❖ Fiber: 2g
- ❖ Sodium: 470mg

Let the slow cooker do the magic as you unwind. This mushroom risotto with fresh herbs and parmesan is not just a meal but a journey to the heart of Italian cuisine. Perfect for a cozy evening, it brings a touch of gourmet to your dinner with ease.

25: Maple Glazed Pork Tenderloin

Savor the succulent flavors of slow-cooked pork tenderloin bathed in a sweet and tangy maple-balsamic glaze. This dish marries the richness of maple syrup with the depth of balsamic vinegar, enhanced by a hint of garlic and a blend of select seasonings.

Servings: 4

Prepping Time: 15 minutes

Cook Time: 4 hours

Difficulty: Easy

Ingredients:

- 1 pork tenderloin (approximately 1 lb)
- 1/2 cup pure maple syrup
- 1/4 cup balsamic vinegar
- 3 cloves garlic, minced
- 1 tablespoon Dijon mustard
- 1 teaspoon dried thyme
- 1/2 teaspoon salt
- 1/4 teaspoon ground black pepper

➢ 2 tablespoons olive oil

Step-by-Step Preparation:

1. In a small bowl, whisk together maple syrup, balsamic vinegar, garlic, mustard, thyme, salt, and pepper.
2. Heat olive oil in a skillet over medium-high heat. Sear the pork tenderloin until golden brown on all sides.
3. Place the seared pork into the slow cooker.
4. Pour the maple-balsamic mixture over the pork in the slow cooker.
5. Cover and cook on low for 4 hours or until the pork is tender.
6. Once cooked, let the pork rest before slicing.
7. Drizzle with the thickened glaze from the slow cooker before serving.

Nutritional Facts: (Per serving)

❖ Calories: 295
❖ Protein: 24g
❖ Carbohydrates: 25g
❖ Fat: 10g
❖ Sodium: 320mg
❖ Sugar: 20g

As the aroma fills your kitchen, this Maple Glazed Pork Tenderloin promises a delightful dining experience. Each tender slice, enriched with the glaze's complexity, will make your slow-cooked dinner the centerpiece of your meal, impressing guests and satisfying your gourmet cravings.

26: Beef Bourguignon Stew

Savor the richness of French cuisine with this slow-cooked beef bourguignon stew. Infused with hearty vegetables and red wine, it's a quintessential comfort food.

Servings: 4

Prepping Time: 20 mins

Cook Time: 6 hrs on low

Difficulty: Medium

Ingredients:

- ➢ 1 lb beef chuck, cut into cubes
- ➢ 2 tbsp all-purpose flour
- ➢ 4 slices bacon, chopped
- ➢ 2 garlic cloves, minced
- ➢ 1 large onion, diced
- ➢ 2 carrots, sliced
- ➢ 2 celery stalks, sliced
- ➢ 8 oz mushrooms, quartered
- ➢ 2 tbsp tomato paste

- ➢ 2 cups red wine
- ➢ 2 cups beef broth
- ➢ 1 bay leaf
- ➢ 1 tsp dried thyme
- ➢ Salt and pepper to taste
- ➢ Fresh parsley for garnish

Step-by-Step Preparation:

1. Toss beef cubes with flour to coat. In the slow cooker, cook bacon until crisp, then remove and set aside.
2. Brown the beef in the bacon fat, then transfer to the slow cooker.
3. Sauté garlic, onions, carrots, and celery until softened; add to the range.
4. Add mushrooms, tomato paste, red wine, beef broth, bay leaf, thyme, salt, and pepper to the field.
5. Cook on low for 6 hours until beef is tender. Garnish with bacon and parsley before serving.

Nutritional Facts: (Per serving)

- ❖ Calories: 480
- ❖ Protein: 35g
- ❖ Carbohydrates: 15g
- ❖ Fat: 20g
- ❖ Sodium: 870mg
- ❖ Fiber: 3g

After hours of slow cooking, this beef bourguignon stew will fill your home with an irresistible aroma, promising a delectable dinner to warm you from the inside out. Bon appétit!

27: Thai Green Curry Chicken

Embrace the flavors of Thailand with this aromatic and creamy Thai Green Curry Chicken, slow-cooked to perfection, allowing spices to meld for an enchanting dining experience.

Servings: 4

Prepping Time: 15 minutes

Cook Time: 4 hours on low

Difficulty: Medium

Ingredients:

- ➢ 1 lb chicken breast, cut into chunks
- ➢ 2 tbsp Thai green curry paste
- ➢ 1 can of coconut milk
- ➢ 1 cup chicken broth
- ➢ 1 bell pepper, sliced
- ➢ 1 small eggplant, cubed
- ➢ 1 tbsp fish sauce
- ➢ 1 tsp brown sugar
- ➢ 1 tbsp vegetable oil

- ➢ 1/2 cup bamboo shoots
- ➢ Fresh basil leaves
- ➢ Salt to taste

Step-by-Step Preparation:

1. Heat the vegetable oil in a pan and sear the chicken until brown.
2. Transfer the chicken to the slow cooker.
3. In the same pan, add green curry paste and a bit of coconut milk; cook for 2 minutes.
4. Pour the mixture over the chicken in the slow cooker.
5. Add coconut milk, chicken broth, bell pepper, eggplant, fish sauce, brown sugar, and bamboo shoots.
6. Stir well, cover, and cook on low for 4 hours.
7. Season with salt and garnish with fresh basil before serving.

Nutritional Facts: (Per serving)

- ❖ Calories: 310
- ❖ Protein: 28g
- ❖ Carbohydrates: 14g
- ❖ Fat: 16g
- ❖ Sodium: 750mg
- ❖ Fiber: 2g

Savor the tender chicken and vegetables infused with the exotic flavors of green curry. This slow cooker Thai Green Curry Chicken is a culinary trip to the heart of Thailand in your kitchen – an effortless creation that's both comforting and refreshing.

28: Greek Lemon Chicken With Potatoes

Embrace the essence of Mediterranean cuisine with this succulent Greek Lemon Chicken with Potatoes. A heavenly slow cooker dish. That promises to tantalize your taste buds with its zesty—and herby flavors, perfect for a comforting family dinner.

Servings: 4

Prepping Time: 15 minutes

Cook Time: 4 hours on high or 7 hours on low

Difficulty: Easy

Ingredients:

- ➤ 4 chicken thighs, bone-in, skin-on
- ➤ 6 medium potatoes, quartered
- ➤ 3 lemons, juiced and zested
- ➤ 4 garlic cloves, minced
- ➤ 2 tbsp olive oil
- ➤ 1 tbsp dried oregano
- ➤ 1 tsp salt
- ➤ ½ tsp black pepper

➢ 1 cup chicken broth
➢ Fresh parsley for garnish

Step-by-Step Preparation:

1. Layer the quartered potatoes at the bottom of the slow cooker.
2. In a bowl, combine lemon juice and zest, garlic, olive oil, oregano, salt, and pepper.
3. Place chicken thighs over potatoes and pour the lemon mixture over the chicken.
4. Add chicken broth to the cooker, cover, and cook on high for 4 hours or on low for 7 hours.
5. Garnish with fresh parsley before serving.

Nutritional Facts: (Per serving)

❖ Calories: 490
❖ Protein: 28g
❖ Carbohydrates: 45g
❖ Fat: 22g
❖ Sodium: 800mg
❖ Fiber: 6g

Conclude your day with a touch of Greek charm. This Greek Lemon Chicken with Potatoes not only fills the room with aromatic herbs and citrus but also fills your evening with ease and delight, letting the slow cooker do all the work for a meal that's as relaxing to make as it is to savor.

29: Duck Breast With Orange Sauce

Indulge in the rich flavors of duck paired with a zesty orange sauce, a dish that promises to tantalize your taste buds with its delightful combination of sweet and savory. Perfect for a cozy dinner, this slow cooker recipe ensures tender, succulent results every time.

Servings: 4

Prepping Time: 20 minutes

Cook Time: 4 hours

Difficulty: Intermediate

Ingredients:

- 4 duck breasts, skin on
- 2 oranges, zest and juice
- 1 tbsp honey
- 1 tsp dried thyme
- 2 cloves garlic, minced
- 1/2 cup chicken broth
- Salt and pepper, to taste
- 1 tbsp olive oil

> ➤ 1 tbsp cornstarch

Step-by-Step Preparation:

1. Season the duck breasts with salt and pepper.
2. In a skillet over medium heat, brown the duck breasts skin-side down until golden.
3. Transfer the duck to the slow cooker.
4. Combine orange zest, juice, honey, thyme, garlic, and broth in a bowl.
5. Pour the mixture over the duck in the slow cooker.
6. Cover and cook on low for 4 hours.
7. Remove the duck and let it rest.
8. Pour sauce into a saucepan, add cornstarch, and simmer until thickened.
9. Slice duck and drizzle with orange sauce.

Nutritional Facts: (Per serving)

- ❖ Calories: 380
- ❖ Protein: 25g
- ❖ Carbohydrates: 15g
- ❖ Fat: 20g
- ❖ Cholesterol: 95mg
- ❖ Sodium: 320mg

As the aroma of duck with orange sauce fills your home, prepare yourself for a luxurious meal that combines ease with elegance. Savor the moments as the slow cooker works its magic, transforming simple ingredients into a gourmet experience that will leave your guests impressed.

30: Beef Stroganoff

Dive into the creamy, tangy depths of Beef Stroganoff, enriched with sour cream and tomato paste, a classic dish made effortlessly in your slow cooker.

Servings: 4

Prepping Time: 15 minutes

Cook Time: 8 hours

Difficulty: Medium

Ingredients:

- 1.5 pounds of beef chuck, sliced into strips
- 1 onion, thinly sliced
- 3 cloves of garlic, minced
- 1 cup of beef broth
- 2 tablespoons of tomato paste
- 1 teaspoon of Dijon mustard
- 1 cup of sour cream
- 2 tablespoons of all-purpose flour
- Salt and pepper to taste
- Chopped parsley for garnish

> ➢ 8 ounces of egg noodles, cooked

Step-by-Step Preparation:

1. Place beef, onions, and garlic in the slow cooker.
2. In a bowl, whisk together beef broth, tomato paste, and Dijon mustard; pour over the beef mixture.
3. Cook on low for 7-8 hours until the beef is tender.
4. Mix flour with sour cream; stir into the slow cooker. Cook on high for an additional 30 minutes.
5. Season with salt and pepper, then serve over cooked noodles and garnish with parsley.

Nutritional Facts: (Per serving)

- ❖ Calories: 500
- ❖ Protein: 35g
- ❖ Carbohydrates: 38g
- ❖ Fat: 24g
- ❖ Saturated Fat: 11g
- ❖ Cholesterol: 140mg
- ❖ Sodium: 420mg
- ❖ Fiber: 3g
- ❖ Sugar: 5g

As your kitchen fills with the aroma of beef simmering in tangy sour cream and tomato, savor the ease of a gourmet slow-cooker meal that promises a comforting end to your day.

Chapter 4: Seafood Siesta Slow Cooker Dishes

31: Spicy Lemon Garlic Shrimp

Indulge in the zesty flavors of Spicy Lemon Garlic Shrimp, a slow cooker delight that effortlessly combines the tang of lemon with the kick of pepper and the aroma of fresh herbs and garlic for a seafood feast.

Servings: 4

Prepping Time: 15 minutes

Cook Time: 3 hours

Difficulty: Easy

Ingredients:

> ➢ 1 lb large shrimp, peeled and deveined
> ➢ 3 cloves of garlic, minced
> ➢ 1 lemon, juice and zest
> ➢ 1/4 cup fresh parsley, chopped
> ➢ 1 teaspoon red pepper flakes
> ➢ 1/2 teaspoon black pepper

➤ 1/4 cup olive oil

➤ Salt to taste

Step-by-Step Preparation:

1. In the slow cooker, whisk together olive oil, lemon juice and zest, garlic, red pepper flakes, and black pepper.
2. Add the shrimp to the mixture and stir to coat evenly.
3. Cover and cook on low for 2.5 to 3 hours.
4. Once cooked, season with salt and garnish with fresh parsley before serving.

Nutritional Facts: (Per serving)

❖ Calories: 215

❖ Protein: 24g

❖ Fat: 11g

❖ Carbohydrates: 3g

❖ Cholesterol: 182mg

❖ Sodium: 117mg

As the slow cooker melds the piquant spices with the juiciness of shrimp, the Spicy Lemon Garlic Shrimp emerges as a testament to the simplicity of slow-cooked elegance. Perfect for a leisurely meal, it's a flavorful journey for your senses.

32: Scallops With Cauliflower Puree

Indulge in the delicate flavors of the sea with this slow cooker recipe for scallops on a bed of creamy cauliflower puree, accented with crispy pancetta sweet green peas, and garnished with micro herbs.

Servings: 4

Prepping Time: 20 mins

Cook Time: 2 hours

Difficulty: Intermediate

Ingredients:

- ➢ 12 large scallops
- ➢ 1 head of cauliflower, cut into florets
- ➢ 100g pancetta, diced
- ➢ 1 cup green peas, fresh or frozen
- ➢ 2 tbsp olive oil
- ➢ Salt and pepper to taste
- ➢ 1/2 cup of milk or cream
- ➢ 1 tbsp butter
- ➢ Micro herbs for garnish

Step-by-Step Preparation:

1. Begin by steaming the cauliflower florets until soft. Then, blend with milk or cream, butter, salt, and pepper to create a smooth puree.
2. In a skillet, cook the pancetta over medium heat until crispy. Remove and set aside.
3. In the same skillet, add a tablespoon of olive oil and sear the scallops for 1-2 minutes on each side until golden brown.
4. Place the scallops in the slow cooker and cook on low for 1.5 hours.
5. In the last 10 minutes of cooking, add the green peas to the slow cooker to warm through.
6. Plate with a spoonful of cauliflower puree, top with scallops, sprinkle over the crispy pancetta and garnish with micro herbs.

Nutritional Facts: (Per serving)

- ❖ Calories: 310
- ❖ Protein: 24g
- ❖ Carbohydrates: 18g
- ❖ Fat: 16g
- ❖ Fiber: 5g
- ❖ Sugar: 5g

As the scallops tenderly cook to perfection in the slow cooker, the harmony of textures and flavors in this dish come together. The crispy pancetta and the fresh pop of green peas elevate the creamy cauliflower puree, making each bite a luxurious experience. Perfect for a cozy night in or a fancy dinner with friends.

33: Cod Stewed With Vegetables

Immerse yourself in the comfort of a slow cooker creation that marries the delicate flavors of cod with a vibrant mix of vegetables and basil; all simmered in a rich tomato sauce. This dish is a testament to the simplicity and heartiness of seafood meals.

Servings: 4

Prepping Time: 15 minutes

Cook Time: 4 hours on low

Difficulty: Easy

Ingredients:

- ➤ 4 cod fillets
- ➤ 2 cups diced tomatoes
- ➤ 1 bell pepper, chopped
- ➤ 1 medium onion, chopped
- ➤ 2 garlic cloves, minced
- ➤ 1/2 cup vegetable broth
- ➤ 2 tablespoons tomato paste
- ➤ 1 teaspoon dried basil

- ➢ Salt and pepper to taste
- ➢ Fresh basil for garnish

Step-by-Step Preparation:

1. Place the onion, bell pepper, and garlic in the bottom of the slow cooker.
2. Top with the cod fillets and sprinkle with salt, pepper, and dried basil.
3. Mix the diced tomatoes with tomato paste and vegetable broth, then pour over the cod.
4. Set the slow cooker to low and cook for approximately 4 hours until the fish is flaky and the vegetables are tender.
5. Garnish with fresh basil before serving.

Nutritional Facts: (Per serving)

- ❖ Calories: 200
- ❖ Protein: 22g
- ❖ Carbohydrates: 10g
- ❖ Fat: 2g
- ❖ Sodium: 300mg
- ❖ Fiber: 2g

Let the slow cooker do the magic as you unwind, and later, delve into a nutritious seafood ensemble that promises to satiate with every spoonful. This cod stew, brimming with basil and tangy tomato sauce, is a love letter to your palate, perfect for any day of the week.

34: Steamed Mussels in Creamy Tomato

Dive into the sumptuous flavors of the sea with this slow cooker steamed mussels in a creamy tomato broth.

Servings: 4

Prepping Time: 15 minutes

Cook Time: 2 hours

Difficulty: Easy

Ingredients:

- ➢ 2 lbs fresh mussels, cleaned and debearded
- ➢ 1 cup tomato sauce
- ➢ 1/2 cup heavy cream
- ➢ 3 cloves garlic, minced
- ➢ 1 small onion, finely chopped
- ➢ 1/2 cup white wine
- ➢ 2 tablespoons fresh parsley, chopped
- ➢ 1 teaspoon red pepper flakes
- ➢ Salt and pepper, to taste

Step-by-Step Preparation:

1. Place the garlic and onion into the slow cooker and pour the tomato sauce and white wine.
2. Season with red pepper flakes, salt, and pepper.
3. Arrange the mussels on top of the sauce.
4. Cover and cook on high for 2 hours.
5. Just before serving, stir in the heavy cream and sprinkle with parsley.

Nutritional Facts: (Per serving)

- ❖ Calories: 310
- ❖ Protein: 22g
- ❖ Carbohydrates: 14g
- ❖ Fat: 16g
- ❖ Cholesterol: 98mg
- ❖ Sodium: 676mg

Savor the richness of this slow-cooked delight where mussels are the star, bathed in a hearty tomato cream sauce. Perfect for a cozy night in, it's a gourmet treat that brings the ocean's freshness to your table with minimal effort.

35: Seafood Gumbo With White Rice

Dive into the deep flavors of the bayou with this hearty seafood gumbo, slow-cooked to perfection and served over fluffy white rice—a symphony of spices and succulent seafood melds in a dish sure to warm your soul.

Servings: 4

Prepping Time: 20 minutes

Cook Time: 4 hours on high

Difficulty: Medium

Ingredients:

- ➢ 1 lb shrimp, peeled and deveined
- ➢ ½ lb crab meat
- ➢ ½ lb andouille sausage, sliced
- ➢ 1 cup okra, sliced
- ➢ 1 large onion, diced
- ➢ 1 green bell pepper, diced
- ➢ 1 cup celery, diced
- ➢ 4 cloves garlic, minced
- ➢ 1 can (14.5 oz) diced tomatoes

- ➤ 4 cups seafood stock
- ➤ 2 tsp Cajun seasoning
- ➤ ½ tsp thyme
- ➤ ½ tsp smoked paprika
- ➤ 2 bay leaves
- ➤ Salt and pepper to taste
- ➤ 2 cups cooked white rice

Step-by-Step Preparation:

1. In your slow cooker, combine onion, bell pepper, celery, garlic, diced tomatoes, and okra.
2. Stir in the seafood stock, Cajun seasoning, thyme, smoked paprika, and bay leaves.
3. Add the sliced andouille sausage to the mixture.
4. Cover and cook on high for 3 hours.
5. Add the shrimp and crab meat and season with salt and pepper. Cook for another hour.
6. Remove bay leaves before serving.
7. Spoon the gumbo over cooked white rice in bowls.

Nutritional Facts: (Per serving)

- ❖ Calories: 450
- ❖ Protein: 35g
- ❖ Carbohydrates: 42g
- ❖ Fat: 15g
- ❖ Cholesterol: 230mg
- ❖ Sodium: 1200mg
- ❖ Fiber: 3g

Savor each spoonful of this slow cooker seafood gumbo, where the blend of spices, tender seafood, and smoky sausage come alive. Each bite takes you closer to the heart of Southern cooking, all from the comfort of your home.

36: Spicy Shrimp Tacos With Coleslaw

Dive into the zest of slow-cooked spicy shrimp tacos paired with crisp coleslaw and tangy salsa for a delightful fusion of flavors.

Servings: 4

Prepping Time: 15 minutes

Cook Time: 2 hours

Difficulty: Medium

Ingredients:

- 1 lb shrimp, peeled and deveined
- 2 cups coleslaw mix
- 1 cup salsa
- 1 tbsp Cajun seasoning
- 2 cloves garlic, minced
- 8 small tortillas
- 1 lime, for garnish
- 1/4 cup fresh cilantro, chopped
- Salt to taste

Step-by-Step Preparation:

1. Season shrimp with Cajun spice and garlic.
2. Place shrimp in the slow cooker on low for 2 hours.
3. Prepare coleslaw mix and set aside.
4. Warm tortillas and set aside.
5. Once shrimp are cooked, assemble tacos with coleslaw and salsa.
6. Garnish with lime wedges and cilantro.

Nutritional Facts: (Per serving)

- ❖ Calories: 350
- ❖ Protein: 24g
- ❖ Carbohydrates: 35g
- ❖ Fat: 12g
- ❖ Fiber: 5g
- ❖ Sodium: 870mg

Wrap up your day with these irresistible slow cooker spicy shrimp tacos, a perfect blend of heat from the shrimp, crunch from the coleslaw, and zest from the salsa.

37: Mediterranean Seafood Stew Cioppino

Dive into the rich flavors of the sea with this slow-cooker Mediterranean Seafood Stew Cioppino. Perfect for any seafood lover looking to warm their soul with a hearty, rustic meal.

Servings: 4

Prepping Time: 20 minutes

Cook Time: 4 hours on high

Difficulty: Medium

Ingredients:

- 1 lb mixed seafood (shrimp, scallops, mussels, and firm fish)
- 1 can (14.5 oz) diced tomatoes
- 1 onion, chopped
- 2 cloves garlic, minced
- 1 bell pepper, diced
- 1 fennel bulb, thinly sliced
- 1/2 cup white wine
- 3 cups seafood stock
- 2 tablespoons tomato paste

- ➢ 1 teaspoon dried oregano
- ➢ 1 teaspoon dried basil
- ➢ 1/2 teaspoon red pepper flakes
- ➢ Salt and pepper to taste
- ➢ 2 tablespoons fresh parsley, chopped
- ➢ 1/4 cup olive oil

Step-by-Step Preparation:

1. Heat olive oil in a skillet over medium heat. Sauté onion, garlic, bell pepper, and fennel until soft.
2. Transfer the sautéed vegetables to the slow cooker.
3. Stir in diced tomatoes, tomato paste, white wine, seafood stock, oregano, basil, and red pepper flakes.
4. Cover and cook on high for 3.5 hours.
5. Add the mixed seafood to the slow cooker, season with salt and pepper, and cook for another 30 minutes.
6. Garnish with fresh parsley before serving.

Nutritional Facts: (Per serving)

- ❖ Calories: 310
- ❖ Protein: 36g
- ❖ Carbohydrates: 18g
- ❖ Fat: 9g
- ❖ Cholesterol: 85mg
- ❖ Sodium: 820mg
- ❖ Fiber: 3g

As the slow cooker works its magic, the aroma of this Mediterranean Seafood Stew Cioppino will transport you to a seaside village. Each spoonful offers a taste of the ocean, with a symphony of spices that will delight your palate.

38: Southern Crawfish Boil

Dive into the heart of Southern cuisine with this slow cooker crawfish boil, brimming with potatoes, sausage, and corn.

Servings: 4

Prepping Time: 20 minutes

Cook Time: 4 hours on high

Difficulty: Easy

Ingredients:

- 2 lbs crawfish, cleaned
- 1 lb andouille sausage, sliced
- 4 medium potatoes, quartered
- 2 ears of corn, halved
- 1 large onion, quartered
- 5 cloves garlic, smashed
- 1 lemon, halved
- 4 tbsp Cajun seasoning
- 2 bay leaves
- 8 cups water

Step-by-Step Preparation:

1. Place potatoes, onions, and garlic at the bottom of the slow cooker.
2. Top with sausage, then corn, and finally crawfish.
3. Squeeze lemon over the top and add the halves into the pot.
4. Sprinkle the Cajun seasoning evenly and add bay leaves.
5. Pour in water, ensuring all ingredients are submerged.
6. Cover and cook on high for 4 hours.
7. Once cooked, drain and serve immediately.

Nutritional Facts: (Per serving)

- ❖ Calories: 390
- ❖ Protein: 35g
- ❖ Carbohydrates: 40g
- ❖ Fat: 12g
- ❖ Sodium: 950mg
- ❖ Fiber: 5g

Wrap up your day with the rich flavors of the South. This slow cooker crawfish boil is not just a meal but an experience, best shared over laughs and good conversation. Enjoy the simplicity of preparation and the complexity of flavors that come together in this timeless Southern delight.

39: Steamed Crabs Fulled

Indulge in the succulent flavors of the sea with this slow-cooked delicacy that brings the essence of coastal cuisine to your table.

Servings: 4

Prepping Time: 20 mins

Cook Time: 4 hours

Difficulty: Medium

Ingredients:

- ➢ 4 giant crabs, cleaned and gutted
- ➢ 2 cups crab meat
- ➢ 4 large eggs
- ➢ 1 tablespoon soy sauce
- ➢ 1 teaspoon sesame oil
- ➢ 1/4 cup chopped green onions
- ➢ 1 teaspoon minced ginger
- ➢ Salt and pepper to taste

Step-by-Step Preparation:

1. In a bowl, mix crabmeat, eggs, soy sauce, sesame oil, green onions, ginger, salt, and pepper.
2. Stuff each crab with the mixture, securing the opening with toothpicks if necessary.
3. Place the crabs in the slow cooker.
4. Cook on low for 4 hours, ensuring they are tender and cooked through.

Nutritional Facts: (Per serving)

- ❖ Calories: 310
- ❖ Protein: 25g
- ❖ Carbohydrates: 2g
- ❖ Fat: 22g
- ❖ Cholesterol: 145mg
- ❖ Sodium: 970mg

After hours of gentle cooking, each crab is perfectly tender, filled with a savory egg blend that's rich in flavor. This slow-cooked seafood feast is sure to impress with its intricate presentation and depth of taste.

40: Parmesan Encrusted Tilapia

Indulge in the delectable fusion of cheese and seafood with our slow cooker Parmesan-encrusted tilapia. This dish promises a savory delight.

Servings: 4

Prepping Time: 15 minutes

Cook Time: 2 hours 30 minutes

Difficulty: Medium

Ingredients:

- ➢ 4 tilapia fillets
- ➢ 1/2 cup grated Parmesan cheese
- ➢ 1/4 cup sliced almonds
- ➢ 2 sprigs of fresh rosemary
- ➢ 1 tablespoon olive oil
- ➢ 1/2 teaspoon garlic powder
- ➢ Salt and pepper to taste

Step-by-Step Preparation:

1. Grease the slow cooker with olive oil.

2. Season the tilapia fillets with salt, pepper, and garlic powder.
3. Place fillets in the slow cooker and sprinkle with grated Parmesan, ensuring an even coat.
4. Scatter sliced almonds over the fillets.
5. Tuck a sprig of rosemary beside each fillet.
6. Cover and cook on low for 2 hours and 30 minutes, or until fish flakes easily with a fork.

Nutritional Facts: (Per serving)

- ❖ Calories: 220
- ❖ Protein: 34g
- ❖ Carbohydrates: 3g
- ❖ Fat: 8g
- ❖ Cholesterol: 55mg
- ❖ Sodium: 210mg

As the slow cooker works magic, the almonds toast gently to a golden crunch while rosemary infuses the tilapia with a subtle, herby fragrance, culminating in a sophisticated yet comforting meal.

Chapter 5: Soup's On Slow Cooker Comfort

41: Creamy Tomato Basil Soup

Indulge in the comforting embrace of homemade Creamy Tomato Basil Soup. This slow cooker recipe ensures a rich, flavorful blend that is perfect for any season.

Servings: 4

Prepping Time: 15 minutes

Cook Time: 6 hours

Difficulty: Easy

Ingredients:

➢ 1 can (28 oz) crushed tomatoes
➢ 1 cup vegetable broth
➢ 1/2 cup chopped fresh basil
➢ 1 teaspoon salt
➢ 1/2 teaspoon black pepper
➢ 1/2 cup heavy cream

➢ 2 cloves garlic, minced
➢ 1 medium onion, diced
➢ 1/4 cup grated Parmesan cheese

Step-by-Step Preparation:

1. Combine tomatoes, broth, garlic, and onion in the slow cooker.
2. Season with salt and pepper.
3. Cover and cook on low for 5-6 hours.
4. Stir in basil and Parmesan cheese.
5. Blend the soup until smooth using an immersion blender.
6. Mix in heavy cream and cook for an additional 15 minutes.
7. Adjust seasoning if necessary.

Nutritional Facts: (Per serving)

❖ Calories: 210
❖ Fat: 14g
❖ Carbohydrates: 18g
❖ Protein: 5g
❖ Sodium: 890mg
❖ Sugars: 12g

Relish the taste of home with this easy-to-make Creamy Tomato Basil Soup. Its slow-cooked richness is the perfect end to any day, promising a delicious, soothing meal that warms the soul.

42: Leeks and Potatoes Soup

Cozy up with this heartwarming slow cooker leek and potato soup infused with the earthy essence of fresh thyme. It's a comfort in a bowl, perfect for chilly days or whenever you crave a simple, rustic meal.

Servings: 4

Prepping Time: 20 minutes

Cook Time: 6 hours

Difficulty: Easy

Ingredients:

- 3 large leeks, cleaned and sliced
- 4 medium potatoes, peeled and diced
- 4 cups vegetable broth
- 2 cloves garlic, minced
- 1 tablespoon fresh thyme, chopped
- 1 teaspoon salt
- ½ teaspoon black pepper
- 1 cup heavy cream
- Chives for garnish

Step-by-Step Preparation:

1. Place leeks, potatoes, and garlic in the slow cooker.
2. Pour in vegetable broth, ensuring the vegetables are covered.
3. Stir in salt, pepper, and fresh thyme.
4. Cover and cook on low for 6 hours until vegetables are tender.
5. Puree the soup using an immersion blender until smooth.
6. Stir in heavy cream and cook on high for an additional 15 minutes.
7. Serve hot, garnished with chives.

Nutritional Facts: (Per serving)

❖ Calories: 310
❖ Protein: 4g
❖ Carbohydrates: 45g
❖ Fat: 12g
❖ Fiber: 5g
❖ Sodium: 890mg

This leek and potato soup showcases the simple elegance of seasonal produce. With its velvety texture and aromatic touch of thyme, it offers solace in every spoonful effortlessly prepared in your slow cooker. Share the warmth with loved ones any day of the week.

43: Chicken Noodle Soup

Savor the home-cooked goodness of chicken noodle soup, enriched with fresh parsley and a medley of vegetables. This slow cooker recipe promises a comforting meal with minimal fuss.

Servings: 4

Prepping Time: 15 minutes

Cook Time: 6 hours

Difficulty: Easy

Ingredients:

- ➤ 1 lb boneless, skinless chicken breasts
- ➤ 6 cups chicken broth
- ➤ 1 cup carrots, chopped
- ➤ 1 cup celery, chopped
- ➤ 1 large onion, diced
- ➤ 3 cloves garlic, minced
- ➤ 2 bay leaves
- ➤ 1 tsp dried thyme
- ➤ Salt and pepper to taste

- ➢ 2 cups egg noodles
- ➢ 1/4 cup fresh parsley, chopped

Step-by-Step Preparation:

1. Place chicken breasts at the bottom of the slow cooker.
2. Add chicken broth, carrots, celery, onion, garlic, bay leaves, thyme, salt, and pepper.
3. Cover and cook on low for 5-6 hours.
4. Remove the chicken, shred it, and return to the slow cooker.
5. Add egg noodles and parsley, and cook on high for another 20 minutes until noodles are tender.

Nutritional Facts: (Per serving)

- ❖ Calories: 350
- ❖ Protein: 27g
- ❖ Carbohydrates: 40g
- ❖ Fat: 7g
- ❖ Sodium: 850mg
- ❖ Fiber: 3g

As the soup simmers to perfection, enjoy the aromas that fill your kitchen. This chicken noodle soup with parsley and vegetables offers a nourishing hug in a bowl, perfect for any day that calls for warmth and wellness.

44: Butternut Squash Apple Soup

Warm up with this cozy butternut squash apple soup, a perfect blend of autumn flavors simmered to perfection in your slow cooker.

Servings: 4

Prepping Time: 20 minutes

Cook Time: 6 hours

Difficulty: Easy

Ingredients:

- 1 medium butternut squash, peeled and cubed
- 2 large apples, peeled, cored, and chopped
- 1 onion, diced
- 3 cups vegetable broth
- 1 cup apple cider
- 1 teaspoon salt
- ½ teaspoon ground cinnamon
- ¼ teaspoon nutmeg
- Freshly ground black pepper, to taste
- 1/2 cup heavy cream (optional)

Step-by-Step Preparation:

1. Place the butternut squash, apples, and onion into the slow cooker.
2. Pour vegetable broth and apple cider, ensuring the mixture covers the vegetables.
3. Season with salt, cinnamon, nutmeg, and black pepper.
4. Cover and cook on low for 6 hours until the squash is tender.
5. Use an immersion blender to puree the soup until smooth.
6. Stir in the heavy cream, if using, and allow to heat through.
7. Serve warm with your choice of garnish.

Nutritional Facts: (Per serving)

- ❖ Calories: 210
- ❖ Protein: 2g
- ❖ Carbohydrates: 50g
- ❖ Fat: 3g
- ❖ Fiber: 6g
- ❖ Sodium: 590mg

Delight in each spoonful of this heartwarming butternut squash apple soup as it offers a comforting embrace, combining the earthy sweetness of squash with the tartness of apple, all from your slow cooker.

45: Creamy Italian Tortellini Wild Rice Soup

Indulge in the comforting embrace of creamy Italian tortellini wild rice soup, brimming with hearty vegetables—a slow cooker marvel that's both nourishing and delightfully simple to prepare.

Servings: 4

Prepping Time: 15 minutes

Cook Time: 6 hours

Difficulty: Easy

Ingredients:

> - 1 cup wild rice blend
> - 4 cups vegetable broth
> - 1 cup chopped carrots
> - 1 cup chopped celery
> - 1 medium onion, diced
> - 3 garlic cloves, minced
> - 1 tsp Italian seasoning
> - 1/2 tsp salt
> - 1/4 tsp black pepper

- ➢ 1 cup heavy cream
- ➢ 2 cups fresh spinach
- ➢ 1 package (9 oz) cheese tortellini
- ➢ 1/2 cup grated Parmesan cheese

Step-by-Step Preparation:

1. Rinse wild rice blend and place in the slow cooker.
2. Add vegetable broth, carrots, celery, onion, garlic, Italian seasoning, salt, and pepper to the range.
3. Cover and cook on low for 5-6 hours or until rice is tender.
4. Stir in heavy cream, spinach, and tortellini.
5. Cover and cook on high for 15 minutes or until tortellini are cooked.
6. Garnish with grated Parmesan cheese before serving.

Nutritional Facts: (Per serving)

- ❖ Calories: 410
- ❖ Protein: 18g
- ❖ Carbohydrates: 50g
- ❖ Fat: 16g
- ❖ Fiber: 4g
- ❖ Sugar: 5g
- ❖ Sodium: 780mg

After a long day, let your slow cooker do the work and come home to a steamy bowl of Italian bliss. This creamy tortellini and wild rice soup is a hug in a bowl, promising to warm your soul with every spoonful.

46: Red Lentils and Tomato Soup

Savor the heartiness of red lentils, barley, and vegetables simmered to perfection in a robust tomato broth. This slow cooker soup is a nourishing and easy-to-prepare meal ideal for any day of the week.

Servings: 4

Prepping Time: 15 minutes

Cook Time: 6 hours on low

Difficulty: Easy

Ingredients:

- ➤ 1 cup red lentils
- ➤ 1/2 cup barley
- ➤ 4 cups vegetable broth
- ➤ 1 can (14 oz) diced tomatoes
- ➤ 2 carrots, diced
- ➤ 2 stalks celery, diced
- ➤ 1 onion, chopped
- ➤ 2 garlic cloves, minced
- ➤ 1 tsp dried thyme

➢ Salt and pepper to taste

Step-by-Step Preparation:

1. Rinse red lentils and barley under cold water.
2. Place lentils, barley, vegetables, and diced tomatoes into the slow cooker.
3. Pour in vegetable broth and add garlic, thyme, salt, and pepper.
4. Stir to combine all ingredients thoroughly.
5. Set the slow cooker on low and cook for 6 hours.
6. Check seasoning and adjust to taste before serving.

Nutritional Facts: (Per serving)

❖ Calories: 320
❖ Protein: 18g
❖ Fiber: 15g
❖ Fat: 1.5g
❖ Sodium: 300mg

After hours of slow cooking, the flavors in this red lentils and tomato soup with barley and vegetables have melded beautifully, creating a comforting and nutritious dish. Perfect for a cozy night in, this soup promises warmth and satisfaction in every spoonful.

47: Beef and Barley Soup

Dive into the hearty goodness of a slow-cooked beef and barley soup, brimming with nourishing vegetables and tender beef. It's the perfect comfort dish for any day of the week.

Servings: 4

Prepping Time: 20 Minutes

Cook Time: 8 Hours

Difficulty: Easy

Ingredients:

➢ 1 lb beef stew meat, cubed
➢ 3/4 cup pearl barley
➢ 4 cups beef broth
➢ 1 cup carrots, chopped
➢ 1 large potato, diced
➢ 1/2 cup celery, chopped
➢ 1/2 cup tomato, diced
➢ 1/2 cup peas
➢ 1 onion, chopped

- ➢ 2 cloves garlic, minced
- ➢ Salt and pepper to taste
- ➢ 2 tbsp olive oil

Step-by-Step Preparation:

1. Heat olive oil in a skillet over medium-high heat. Add beef cubes and cook until browned.
2. Place the browned beef, barley, broth, carrots, potato, celery, tomato, peas, onion, and garlic into the slow cooker.
3. Season with salt and pepper.
4. Stir to combine all the ingredients well.
5. Cover and cook on low for 8 hours until the beef is tender and the barley is cooked.

Nutritional Facts: (Per serving)

- ❖ Calories: 350
- ❖ Protein: 24g
- ❖ Carbohydrates: 45g
- ❖ Fat: 8g
- ❖ Fiber: 9g
- ❖ Sodium: 700mg

After hours of slow cooking, your beef and barley soup is ready to envelop you in its warm embrace. Each spoonful is a testament to the simplicity of ingredients transforming into a dish that tastes like home.

48: Corn Chowder Soup With Bacon

Indulge in the creamy richness of Corn Chowder Soup, brought to life with savory bacon—a comfort in every spoonful effortlessly prepared in your slow cooker.

Servings: 4

Prepping Time: 15 minutes

Cook Time: 6 hours on low

Difficulty: Easy

Ingredients:

- ➤ 4 slices bacon, chopped
- ➤ 4 cups corn kernels, fresh or frozen
- ➤ 1 diced onion
- ➤ 2 diced carrots
- ➤ 2 diced celery stalks
- ➤ 1 minced garlic clove
- ➤ 4 cups chicken broth
- ➤ 1 cup heavy cream
- ➤ 1 teaspoon thyme

- ➤ Salt and pepper to taste
- ➤ 2 diced potatoes
- ➤ Chopped chives for garnish

Step-by-Step Preparation:

1. In a skillet, cook bacon until crisp; transfer to a paper towel-lined plate.
2. Place corn, onion, carrots, celery, garlic, potatoes, thyme, salt, pepper, and chicken broth in the slow cooker.
3. Cover and cook on low for 6 hours until vegetables are tender.
4. Stir in heavy cream and half of the bacon; cook for another 15 minutes.
5. Serve garnished with remaining bacon and chives.

Nutritional Facts: (Per serving)

- ❖ Calories: 450
- ❖ Total Fat: 22g
- ❖ Saturated Fat: 12g
- ❖ Cholesterol: 70mg
- ❖ Sodium: 950mg
- ❖ Total Carbohydrates: 50g
- ❖ Dietary Fiber: 5g
- ❖ Sugars: 10g
- ❖ Protein: 15g

As the aroma fills your home, savor the soul-warming flavors of this Corn Chowder Soup. Each bite, dotted with crispy bacon and tender vegetables, promises a cozy culinary hug, perfect for any slow-cooked meal gathering.

49: Classic French Onion Soup

Savor the heartwarming flavors of France with this classic French onion soup. Rich, caramelized onions meld with a robust beef broth, topped with a golden crust of Gruyère and toasted baguette.

Servings: 4

Prepping Time: 15 minutes

Cook Time: 6 hours

Difficulty: Medium

Ingredients:

- ➢ 4 large yellow onions, thinly sliced
- ➢ 2 cloves of garlic, minced
- ➢ 4 cups of beef broth
- ➢ 2 tablespoons of unsalted butter
- ➢ 1 teaspoon of sugar
- ➢ 1 bay leaf
- ➢ 1/2 teaspoon of dried thyme
- ➢ Salt and freshly ground black pepper to taste
- ➢ 1/2 cup of white wine

> ➤ 4 slices of baguette, toasted
> ➤ 1 cup of shredded Gruyère cheese

Step-by-Step Preparation:

1. In the slow cooker, melt the butter and add onions, garlic, sugar, salt, and pepper. Cook on high until onions are translucent.
2. Stir in thyme, bay leaf, and white wine. Cook for 10 minutes.
3. Add beef broth and set the cooker on low for 6 hours.
4. Preheat the broiler. Ladle soup into oven-safe bowls.
5. Top each with a slice of toasted baguette and Gruyère cheese.
6. Broil until cheese is bubbly and golden brown.
7. Serve immediately.

Nutritional Facts: (Per serving)

- ❖ Calories: 350
- ❖ Protein: 15g
- ❖ Carbohydrates: 44g
- ❖ Fat: 12g
- ❖ Sodium: 870mg
- ❖ Fiber: 4g

Relish the culmination of your culinary efforts as each spoonful of this sumptuous French onion soup gratifies your taste buds. The slow-cooked onions and melted Gruyère cheese create a symphony of flavor, making this dish a timeless comfort classic.

50: Chicken Tortilla Soup

Dive into the heartwarming flavors of this slow cooker Chicken Tortilla Soup. A perfect blend of spices, chicken, and tortillas simmered to perfection, it's a comforting meal for any day of the week.

Servings: 4

Prepping Time: 15 minutes

Cook Time: 4 hours on high or 7 hours on low

Difficulty: Easy

Ingredients:

- ➢ 1 lb boneless, skinless chicken breasts
- ➢ 1 (15 oz) can black beans, rinsed and drained
- ➢ 1 (14.5 oz) can diced tomatoes
- ➢ 1 large onion, chopped
- ➢ 1 bell pepper, chopped
- ➢ 1 jalapeño, seeded and minced
- ➢ 2 cloves garlic, minced
- ➢ 4 cups chicken broth
- ➢ 1 cup frozen corn

- ➢ 1 tsp chili powder
- ➢ 1 tsp cumin
- ➢ Salt and pepper to taste
- ➢ 1 cup tortilla strips or crushed tortilla chips
- ➢ Fresh cilantro and sliced avocado for garnish

Step-by-Step Preparation:

1. Place the chicken breasts at the bottom of the slow cooker.
2. Add black beans, diced tomatoes, onion, bell pepper, jalapeño, and garlic.
3. Pour chicken broth and sprinkle chili powder, cumin, salt, and pepper.
4. Cover and cook on high for 4 hours or low for 7 hours.
5. Remove the chicken, shred it with two forks, and return to the pot.
6. Stir in frozen corn and continue to cook for an additional 30 minutes.
7. Serve hot, topped with tortilla strips, cilantro, and avocado slices.

Nutritional Facts: (Per serving)

- ❖ Calories: 350
- ❖ Protein: 28g
- ❖ Carbohydrates: 33g
- ❖ Fiber: 7g
- ❖ Fat: 9g
- ❖ Sodium: 870mg

This Chicken Tortilla Soup is not just a meal; it's a warm embrace in a bowl. Each spoonful is a taste of home, infused with the ease of your slow cooker. Enjoy this no-fuss, hearty soup, and let it become your go-to for busy days and cozy nights.

Conclusion

As we draw the curtains on this delicious journey through "Tasty Easy Slow Cooker Recipes With Pictures," we hope that Linda Lizzie's collection has not only filled your kitchen with irresistible aromas but also equipped you with an arsenal of dishes that span from heartwarming classics to modern twists on traditional fare.

Each recipe has been crafted carefully, ensuring you can embrace the joys of home cooking without the stress. Linda's step-by-step instructions, accompanied by vivid photographs, have been designed to guide you through the cooking process, making each dish accessible regardless of your culinary expertise.

The magic of a slow cooker is its ability to transform simple ingredients into something extraordinary with little effort from you, the cook. It's our sincerest wish that this book becomes a well-thumbed favorite in your digital library, dog-eared and annotated with your notes and memories as you revisit these recipes time and again.

Remember that the heart of slow cooking is patience and simplicity. As you continue to explore the recipes Linda Lizzie has shared, may you also discover moments of connection and comfort around your table. Whether it's a busy weekday dinner or a leisurely weekend feast, these slow-cooker meals will satisfy and inspire.

Thank you for inviting "Tasty Easy Slow Cooker Recipes With Pictures" into your home and kitchen. Keep it close for days when you crave the simplicity and warmth of a home-cooked meal, and let your slow cooker do the work while you savor the rich, deep flavors that only time can weave.

Printed in Great Britain
by Amazon